Acing the Admissions Essay

MARK S. MOONEY

DEDICATION

This book is dedicated to all of my students, past and present, for their genius, creativity, and inspiration.

CONTENTS

ACKNOWLEDGMENTS

First and foremost, I want to thank all of my former students for their willingness to share their essays as models and as inspiration to those that follow. These students are amazing! Their essays are amazing! I don't know anyone who doesn't ooh and aw over Haoxiaohan Cai's essay about her name or Lauren Wilson's story-telling essay. All of the samples included here provide a gamut of ideas for enrapturing the body and soul of a student applicant. I am very proud to call them my students.

Further, I want to thank Jiyoon Cho for helping me with editing and putting the finishing touches on the book. As a student who recently went through this entire process herself, Jiyoon was an incredible help. I also want to thank Mackenzie Moreno for her unselfish assistance in getting the book to print. I thank all of my students for sharing their gifts.

Thank you as well to Lisa Finn for helping provide suggestions for the second edition of the book, and its marketing.

I hope that this book will assist you in gaining admission into the college of your choice, and help you tell your story. Best wishes on your journey!

Semper Fidelis,

Mark S. Mooney

1

INTRODUCTION

When the college admissions committee receives your application, you don't want to just be a number produced from a formula. Your SAT score, no matter how good or bad, cannot possibly represent all of you. Your class rank, even if you're number one of one thousand, or four-hundred and twenty-one of one thousand, cannot possibly represent all of you. Your Grade Point Average, whether it is 4.49, or 2.49, cannot possibly represent all of you either. You have a life beyond SATs, GPAs, and class rankings. And with that life, you have stories. Now all of those stories cannot possibly be told in one college admissions essay, or even two essays, but through one or two poignant stories, the admissions committee will get a glimpse, a personal experience, or an anecdote that will give insight into who YOU are.

They will read something to remember.

So, with all of that data: SAT, GPA, class rank, SAT-II's, AP scores, and the list goes on, they can take those *stories* and get to know the person behind those numbers. Through your college essays, you can transform yourself from a number, to a person. And hopefully you'll be a person they'd like to have at their university.

Colleges and universities want a diverse student body. They don't want everyone to think the same, participate in the same activities, and have the same values or have the same interests. Everyone has done something unique. And that is one of the goals of the essay: to reveal you as a unique person, and not just a statistic.

As a freshman at Boston University, I was walking through the halls during freshman orientation, and suddenly a lady stopped me and said hello. She knew my name and she introduced herself as Dr. Marilyn Root, the Assistant Dean of the College of Communication. Then she told me how she enjoyed reading about my experience as a military journalist in Spain. How did she know any of this? From my college essays? *What*? I thought to myself. *Someone actually reads those things. Someone actually remembered who I was from my essay.* Well, it was true, and it is still true today. The college essay can be memorable and should be memorable. And it should help you get into the college best suited for you.

Now as a high school teacher for over a decade, I have read hundreds upon hundreds of college essays, trying to help students tell their stories, and trying to help students get into the best colleges. Furthermore, as an AP English Teacher, I have been fortunate to have a diverse and talented collection of students, and I have written hundreds of letters of recommendations. These students have gone on to be accepted into places such as: Harvard, Yale, and Stanford, but many others have been accepted into places like the University of Michigan, Boston College, Northwestern, the University of San Diego, Baylor, the University of Colorado, and the list goes on. The one thing that they could control was their essays. The one thing that you can control is your essays. And so I offer this book to you, to help you write the best college essays, and to help you get into the best college. Take notes in the book, write down ideas in the margin, and let the journey begin. Good luck!

2

THE ONE THING UNDER YOUR CONTROL

Almost every university in the country receives more applicants than they can admit. Keep in mind throughout the time you put in working on the college essays, that your time and effort will pay off. As I said before, the essay is the one thing under your control. Let me give you a few examples of schools with a lot of applicants. Over 55,000 students applied to the University of California, Los Angeles (UCLA) in 2008, according to the UCLA Office of Analysis and Information Management. Guess how many were accepted. Twenty thousand? Fifteen thousand? Not quite. Only 12,660 got in (22%), and only a mere 4,735 entered UCLA as freshman. Okay, I'll admit UCLA is one of the most applied to schools in the country, if not THE most applied to school in the country depending on the year. Then let's take another example: Northwestern. Over 25,000 applied to Northwestern in 2008, and 26% were accepted – slightly higher than UCLA. So, if everyone applying to schools like these has a high GPA and has been president of this club or that club, and everyone got an SAT tutor, etc. what is the one thing that can make the difference? That's right: the admissions essay. I want you to get into the school of your choice. You are already on the right track by reading this book while many of your friends will wing it, and submit their essays the night before they are due. So, I commend you on taking the smart approach.

Some people say the process of writing the essay may help you learn about yourself. This is especially important during the brainstorming process. I agree to an extent, but I also believe that the process of writing will allow you to *sell* yourself to the school. This does not mean that you present yourself as something you're not. Don't pretend to be a mental giant by using pedantic diction. Don't pretend to be Jesus or Buddha or Gandhi or some completely unselfish philanthropic person if that is not who you really are. Be yourself. Present yourself. Whether you're applying to Tufts University or Tulane, it does not matter. Each school is looking for a diverse student body. You can get in by being yourself. You don't have to be the next prodigy. You already know if you are a prodigy or not. You already know a lot about yourself. You just need to start reflecting and processing what you know about yourself and get it down on paper.

Moreover, you already have the credentials and you already have taken most of the tests you will need to get accepted. Now the next step is to use your essay to augment information not already on the application. Additionally, if your grades and class ranking weren't as high as you had hoped for, your essay can push you over the top. Many admissions committees are open to the smart, creative, or unique student who has a lower GPA, etc. but might actually represent a diamond in the rough. When I was at Boston University, the guy across the hall from me had about a 2.1 GPA. That's pretty awful, as I'm sure you'll agree. So how did he get in? Firstly, he scored in the 90th percentile on the SAT, and secondly, in his essay he wrote about being a sushi chef for two summers before he even graduated from high school. That's a great story and it was a great essay. That's how he got in. That's unique.

The essay can be used for a variety of purposes. You can use your essay to explain some of the less favorable aspects of yourself. (Let's say

12

you had low grades as a freshman for instance. (Something like: "I struggled my freshman year in high school largely due to my parent's divorce and my move to a new high school..." will help tell your story). Regardless of your story or your situation, everyone needs to do their best on the essays. Even a superstar with a 4.6 GPA and a 2300 SAT can be rejected by a good school, if their essays are blasé and don't really show anything about the applicant other than what they couldn't read on their application – that they are smart. Trust me, there are a lot of "smart" 17- and 18-year-olds applying to colleges these days. You want to assert yourself as someone who is unique. You *are* unique, after all. So it should be easy. One admissions officer I spoke to put it this way: "We like the Eagle Scouts, but we like the comedians too." I'll say this again: colleges want a mix of students.

3

RESEARCHING THE COLLEGE

You are applying to specific colleges for specific reasons, I am sure. As part of your preparation to write the college admissions essays, you should do some deeper research of the colleges. Though it may seem like a no-brainer, start by looking at the tips and suggestions the college offers for their essays. Look through the college website with scrutiny. After you have examined their tips and suggestions, then look more broadly at the school's history. Think about the school's philosophy. Find out who some famous alumni are. One of the reasons I chose Boston University for my undergraduate work was because, at the time, Saul Bellow and Elie Wiesel were professors there. I was interested in writing, so having great writers teach there was a big draw.

Think back to your campus tour, if you took one. What made this school unique? Why would you choose this school over all of the others? You may want to convey that uniqueness in your essay. College admissions officers want to know why you want to go their college – as opposed to the hundreds upon hundreds of others. An admissions officer from Boston University said this about applicants who might be "on the fence" so to speak, for acceptance or rejection: "Many times we'll go after second semester grades, the short answer questions, and the essays. We read the essay on *why* you want to come to Boston University."

I recommend you talk to current students of the college, if you know any. They are a great resource. Ask them what they think makes the college unique? This might not only help you write your essay, but it may help you decide if you even want to apply there. This will all help in building background knowledge before you start brainstorming ideas about yourself that you want to convey in the essays.

Assignment: Go online and print off the essay topics included in the applications for each of the colleges or universities you are interested in applying to. You may notice that some of the essays are in "common" and others are completely unique to the school. This will also give you a glimpse as to what kind of work lies ahead. (Oh, by the way: this could be the first step in cutting down the number of schools you plan on applying to, as well.)

4

BRAINSTORMING

Okay, now that we've established that the essays are really important and that they can make an important difference in your admission to whatever school you want to get into, let's talk about getting started. I recommend that you start this process at least by July or August of your senior summer, but if it's the week before your essays are due, and you are just getting started with reading this book as fast as you can before you crank out nine essays over nineteen coffees or sodas, then so be it. The only reason I recommend you start a few months early is because it's nice to be able to really think about what's important to you: what's important about you, and what's the most important thing you'd like to say. A lot of the essays only give you 250 or 500 words, and you can't possibly encapsulate your entire life story in that short amount of space, so you have to be selective. Consequently, that selectivity has to start somewhat broad and then be narrowed down and focused. That's right: you have to start just like you did for that 11th grade essay on something "descriptive as hell" that Stradlater was supposed to write but Holden Caulfield wrote for him. You have to brainstorm. Now, I hope you are not going to throw this essay away like Holden did, but if you do have to throw the first draft away, that's okay: you're brainstorming.

This can actually be really fun. It's a great chance to look back at some of the many things you have done over the span of your high school career and your life. It is also a great chance to look ahead into the future and think about where you want to be and what you want to be doing. So, don't hold back, don't hesitate to write anything and everything down. This is NOT the time to overanalyze. There is no bad idea and there is no unimportant event or accomplishment. Write them all down. Don't be afraid to write down unusual or funny ideas. Think of it as a stream of consciousness activity; once you start just keep going and eventually there will be an essay topic in there. Go through each of the suggested brainstorming activities in this chapter. Take your time if you can. I would recommend no more than two lists or activities a day. You may want to start one and then think about it for the day, while you're at the beach or the lake, or while you're driving to a friend's house. You never know what idea or event could become the perfect essay topic. It will come.

Top Schools

Write down the schools you are interested in applying to. It's a good idea to list 1 or 2 "dream schools" as well as a couple of "safety schools." Someone may have told you that you're a "shoe in," but it is wiser to keep all of your options open.

Indiana University
Parsons
FIT
Utah University

DREAM
Central Saint Martins
NYU
USC

Now your homework (if you didn't already do this in the chapter on Researching the College) is to go online and look up the essay prompts and supplements for each college or university listed. You may also want to find something you would want to participate in at the school to make the school's essays easier to brainstorm. (e.g. Boston University, Common Application). While you are looking up each school, list all of the prompts to see which ones can overlap. (You don't want to write 18 essays if you can write 8 instead, do you?)

Five Years Ago

Think back to four or five years ago. List experiences, problems, memories, and any lasting impressions from the past. One of these incidents, could have been life-changing...you never know.

Five Years from Now

Try to imagine where you want to be five years from now. Will you be earning a Master's Degree, at the start of medical school or law school, or will you be in the work force? What is your goal? What would be your dream job after college? Or will you have started your own business by then? List as many things as you can imagine that you will have achieved in five years. Consider academic achievements as well.

-Dancing with a ballet company or major in dance

*Dream Companies

- ABT
- RNZB
- Dutch National
- Batsheva
- Ballet West

- degree in Fashion Design

- start a clothing label or earning an internship with a high end company

- study abroad

*living in NY

Twenty Years from Now

Now, take it one step further. Will you be a Vice President somewhere. Where will you live? Will you have branches of your own company all over America or the globe? Will you have invented a new product, like the iPhone or the bluetooth or something for the kitchen or the office? Maybe you'll accidentally leave some glue on a piece of paper: you've just invented the post it. Or maybe you have your eyes set on a more traditional route? Will you be a professor or an architect? Doctor or nurse? Lawyer or legal writer? Dentist or dermatologist? Dream big and write some of those big dreams and ideas down on paper.

— Principal Dancer or professional dancer at dream company

— own a ~~xxxx~~ clothing company in New York

— own a penthouse

— adopt 2 kids

— have 2 dogs 2 cats

— marry rich

~~xxxxxxxxxx~~

— spend most $ on travel

Teachers & Coaches

List all of your favorite teachers and coaches since the 1st grade. Of course you won't remember all of them. The goal is to write down just the favorites. Was there a 2nd grade teacher who inspired you to become an avid reader? How about a track or golf coach who took you under his or her wing? Did your music teacher inspire you to be the best? List them all. Write down your most influential family members as well: Uncle Stan or your "God Father." Try to list 8 or 10.

Mrs. Dennis   Mrs. Schmidke

*Ms Rika

Ms. Alaine

Ms. Kelly

Ms. Willett

Mr. Easter

Ms. Amanda

Ms. Heather

Ms. Kathleen

Ms. Jaclyn

Allison & Rex

Mr. B

Ms. McMichael

Now next to each "influential person" try to jot down a story or anecdote which demonstrates how they influenced you.

Awards, Accomplishments, & Honors

List all of the awards you can think of as far back as you can remember. If you can, look through your past folders and look through clippings your mom or dad might have saved. Did you win the spelling bee in the 2nd grade? Did you win a high school Academic Decathlon award? Student of the month? Rotary speech winner? Don't hesitate – just list.

- Cricket Magazine
- Top Scientist 101
- first summer intensive
- torch of exellence

Now next to each award or accomplishment, try to jot down a story or anecdote which ties in with that accomplishment. Perhaps the award was "Most Improved" in orchestra or tennis: write down a story that you can remember about that year or season.

Creative Kick

Personal Triumphs & Challenges

Try to list as many challenges you've had in your life. How did you handle them? Perhaps your mom was hospitalized or your parents went through a divorce or you were in a car accident. Don't rule any out: no matter how big or small, write down every challenge in your life the last 4 or 5 years. What did you learn from the experience? Try to personalize what you went through. How did the situation make you feel? How did you adjust? (i.e. something you tried really hard at and failed, or you tried hard and succeeded...)

- I got declined to PTD at first but worked my ass off for next two weeks to earn it
- anxiety issues

Journal Topic #1

Take a few minutes to think about your past: how are you different now than you were 2-3 years ago? What caused that change? Were you really shy as an 8th or 9th grader and now you have come out of your shell? Were you cocky as an 8th grader and you matured into a humble but confident senior?

Journal Topic #2

Qualities You Like About Yourself

Write down all of the qualities you like about yourself. Don't be humble.
Or if that's a quality, write it down – along with about 10 or 15 others.

- hardworking
- different / individual
- creative
- independent / introvert
- overachiever
- kind
- supportive / encouraging
- determined
- future focussed

Now next to each quality, jot down a story or anecdote that supports the
quality you just described.

- journey to become professional ballet
dancer — give up summer

wake up early to run

gave up high school

take pilates before ballet

4 hrs. a day

Journal Topic #3

Qualities You Did NOT Like About Yourself…but Have Improved

Write down all of the qualities you did not like about yourself. Then next to them write down how you have tried to improve. One of these could be a great story about personal growth.

- low self confidence
  tell myself something
  positive in mirror
  daily

- introvert
  talk to friends

- impulse / talk too much

- ~~saad~~ eat gross   - stubborn
- boring   - rude
- obsessive   - ANXIETY
- people hate me   WOOO
- body type
- self oriented
- annoying
- hurt others

Just as before, next to each quality, you should have a story or anecdote that supports the growth and improvement you just described.

5

ORGANIZING AND WRITING THE ESSAY

Is *what* you say in your admissions essay necessarily more important than *how* you say it? There is no wrong or right answer to that question. They are both important. They both have equal merit. Now listen, if you have done at least some of the activities that I have recommended at this point, then you have spent a LOT of time brainstorming, listing, thinking, talking, and deciding WHAT to write about. So, make sure you do your best job actually writing it. Sometimes, if one of the topics for one essay isn't as strong as the other one, the essay can be just as powerful if it is powerfully written. Here are some things to consider:

Fritz Kuhlenz from Boston University Admissions says, "Writing style is important to a certain extent. We're looking at the story and the style. Some students are going to have amazing experiences like a safari in Africa or something so it's easier for them to relate the story. Other kids will write about a campfire in the backyard with their family, and that can be good too. An essay that is eloquent, unique, and clearly written will give it an added boost." That added "boost" is what we want to focus on.

Your essay does not need to be a "five paragraph essay" like you were taught in the 8ᵗʰ grade. Your essay can be as short as three paragraphs or as long as six or seven or eight paragraphs. It depends on a lot of things. The paragraph is the main unit of composition. Each paragraph should have one central idea. The essay as a whole should promote one central idea. The sentences do not all have to be compound-complex twenty to thirty words. In fact, they should not be. That is boring; that is monotonous; you do not want to be boring and monotonous. See what I mean? You want sentence variety and variety in paragraph structure. Mix it up a little.

Don't be afraid of the one sentence paragraph.

To make a point stronger, you may want to separate one sentence by itself. You may also want to make a point in just a two or three sentence paragraph. You may also need seven or eight sentences to tell the story of your work at a nearby homeless shelter. It may take that many sentences for you to synthesize your ideas on Lincoln's speeches and how those speeches inspired you to want to apply to be a communications major or a rhetoric major at Boston University or Harvard. There is no formula for sentences or paragraphs in an admissions essay.

I want to demonstrate one sample of creative organization by one of my former students.

How did the world you grew up in shape your dreams and aspirations?

By Lauren Wilson, Stanford University Class of 2013

I have a story for you.

In a land far far away, a lively little Vietnamese girl wreaked havoc with her impish antics. She peed in the clogs of girls she didn't like at school and sometimes even stained their dresses with bright red ink. Well-to-do girls like her attended private schools; the only real contact she had with the opposite sex took place within her family, yet somehow, she managed to sustain a relationship with her secret boyfriend. Correspondence was difficult. She walked home from school each day with an open book in her arms. Her sweetheart rode by on his bike and, in one perfectly timed second, dropped a love letter into her book. She snapped it shut immediately to protect his adoring words until she found a safe moment to read them.

Grandma was my nonfiction.

Once upon a time, there lived a werewolf. He was the friendly, civilized type if such a type existed – held a steady job, lived peacefully with his family in the suburbs, loved golf. It took him until his mid-forties to discover his mystical powers. His new appetite compelled him to gobble voracious amounts of the finest filet mignon and quench his thirst with equally excellent blood red wine. He took his wife and half-werewolf children on car rides during which he and his progeny would howl lustily at full harvest moons. The yellow of the celestial sphere would tinge my mother's face orange – the golden moonbeams blending with the tomato red of her embarrassment.

Dad was my original fiction.

She lived happily ever after, but it certainly didn't start that way. At sixteen, she escaped from Vietnam with her siblings on a small fishing boat meant for ten people, not the fifty smashed together like cheap sardines. Even after she made it through various refugee camps in the Philippines and Malaysia, life was still hard, especially as a teenager alone in a foreign country forced to act as a mother to her siblings. It took nearly a decade from the time she left her home country before she finally found happiness and stability with my dad.

Mom was my historical nonfiction.

Their words wove elaborate nets of vivid imagery, broken English, hilarity, amusement, fury, and sometimes even touching poignancy. My predilection for stories goes beyond the traditional bedtime tale and permeates every aspect of my existence. Each tale I glean becomes another page in the enormous tome of my life.

Now I tell stories of my own. Crazy adventures with friends involving killer skunks and 4 a.m. Denny's stops, family vacations gone awry, awkward school dances, unrequited crushes, I file each one into my mental rolodex just waiting for the opportune time to unleash my tales. I want to fill my life with them, to create my own story by telling the stories of others. The best stories need no embellishing; they just happen, unfold, occur – daily occurrences, world affairs waiting to be translated into print. Flipping fiercely through the flimsy pages searching for my latest article, I wear black ink smudges on my palms proudly; the thrill of sharing my stories expunges any fatigue. Storytelling is my natural high. I bring stories to life and they give me something to live for.

Evaluation:

In terms of structure and organization, this is one of the most creative essays that I have seen. And though Lauren's credentials were very impressive, I have no doubt that this essay helped her gain admission to many of the top universities in the country. From the very beginning, she grabs the reader's interest with concrete details and her mature prose. The reader imagines her grandmother peeing in the "clogs of girls she didn't like at school." It's humorous and compelling. Every single sentence paragraph ("Grandma was my nonfiction") separates the characters in her essay, and transitions the reader to someone new. It's powerful. It's telling. And it provides a great voice for her family and herself. The reader finishes in awe of her stories of family members, in awe of her writing ability, and naturally in awe of the applicant. Her vocabulary is high level ("poignancy," "predilection," and "unrequited") yet it is not forced or showy. And she employs the active voice; there is nothing passive about this essay.

It is no wonder that Lauren was accepted into Stanford University.

6

WRITING WITH STYLE

How you write can really contribute to the success of your essay. Since you have done all of this brainstorming, and all of this listing, and you have finally narrowed it down to a few subjects, or just a few "significant" experiences, now you want to make sure you do your best to articulate that experience. If you have never done so, I would recommend you read *The Elements of Style* by Strunk and White. You can read that book in just a few sittings and it can really be a great guide to your style. If you don't have time to read it, that's okay. Don't panic. I'm sure you have already developed a solid writing style at this point in your life; however, we all have room for improvement. I will give you a few brief pointers here.

We've already alluded to the idea of stretching yourself as a writer through creative organization, as in Lauren's essay on her world. In addition to being creative with your structure, I recommend you use at least a few of these rhetorical devices:

> ➢ **Figurative language**: A powerful metaphor can illustrate a point about your life or your character as an applicant, or convey to the reader the complexity and eloquence of

your writing – while still being clear. (See Lauren's packed like "cheap sardines" example.) Figurative language could come in the form of an extended metaphor such as the United Nations in Helen Cai's essay or Nikki Mello's color essay (see Chapter 10).

➤ **Parallelism**: To repeat the same word or phrase at the beginning (or the end) of successive phrases can add cadence to your writing, as you build up to a major point or life epiphany. This epiphany should be true. This epiphany should be telling. This epiphany should be influential. (See what I mean?)

➤ **Vary sentence length & structure**: Again, most students will write sentences that are roughly 25-30 words, but I recommend you intersperse a few short simple declaratives. This can be powerful. Also, use listing or the much longer, compound-complex sentence when you're trying to extend an idea or to mirror the extension of time in an event.

➤ **Use the active voice**: Another great aspect of Lauren's essay and of many other essays, is the active voice. She doesn't just *tell* us about her grandparent's past lives; she brings her grandparents to life.

➤ **Use concrete details**: The more concrete and the more descriptive your essay, the more memorable your essay will be to the members of the admissions committee. You've probably heard your English teacher say a thousand times: **SHOW vs. tell**. Don't just tell them that you volunteer at a homeless shelter. Show them what it smells like, what the food tastes like, and what the man you met looks like in detail. (See Lauren's peeing in the "clogs" or "blood red wine" examples.)

➤ **Employ symbolism &/or the extended metaphor**: Check out Krista Ward's couch essay in Chapter 8. It's all about her couch, but it's NOT all about her couch. It's a symbol, and a good symbol tied to who you are as a person can be both creative and revealing to the admissions reader. In addition, the **extended metaphor** can also be an amazing tool to make your essay stand out, and to make YOU stand out – more importantly. Read Helen Cai's essay all about "Helentopia" in Chapter 7. It's a different world! Some books will say DON'T do the extended metaphor. I disagree. Just don't overdo it, don't be cliché, and don't let the metaphor take the focus off of revealing the type of person you are to the college admissions committee. (Remember: high risk, high reward!)

> **End with a powerful denouement**: The last thing the admissions officer reads needs to make a lasting impression. Whether you decide to go for a more creative approach to writing your essay, or you decide to go for a more direct approach, you need to tie it all together in the end. It doesn't need to be wrapped in a neat bow, as the cliché goes, but it does need to make the reader pause and think: wow, this student put some thought into this. If you need motivation, read Haoxiaohan Cai's name essay in the "Diversity and You" section of Chapter 8. See if she impresses you at all with her conclusion.

7

HIGH RISK: HIGH REWARD

You don't want to be banal in your approach to the essay. An essay that starts off, "the quality I most like about myself is"....is going to put the reader to sleep! There are some great and some very original ways to write your essay. That's what we're looking for: originality. You are original. Don't tell the admissions office you want to write a book some day: give them an excerpt from the book. Look back at Lauren Wilson's essay. It doesn't go right into answering a prompt by saying, "I believe my family history shaped who I am today...." It's not a stereotypical topic sentence like something you'd write for your freshman English teacher's biographical essay assignment. It's fresh. It's original. She took a little bit of a risk, and it paid off big. You can do the same thing. You don't want to start your essay with some over-used quote from a song by the Beatles, or a quote from Gandhi about being the change in the world. Be yourself. They want to read *your* story – not quotes from other people. The risk can come in the form of organization, extended metaphor, or humor – just make sure it's appropriate. Brainstorm. Free write. Journal.

Whatever it takes – the idea is inside of you; you just need to get it down on paper.

One summer I was sitting with Helen Cai, one of my top students, at the library and we were doing exactly what I was just talking about: brainstorming ideas for her essay. We were focused on the "your world" essay that is one of the two mandatory essays for the University of California system. For 2009, the prompt said: "Describe the world you come from — for example, your family, community or school — and tell us how your world has shaped your dreams and aspirations." It's really a great prompt, but at the time we did not have any great ideas. She really wanted to use a metaphor to describe her family, so that's what we were focused on. Since Helen was really into Model United Nations (MUN), her idea was to somehow incorporate that into a metaphor for her mom, dad, and sister. I told her I loved the idea.

Now we both agreed that a lot of students were in MUN, and a lot of students might talk about MUN in an essay, so we had to do something different. I remember Helen saying, "As long as it is unique, even if it's a bit quirky, then it will be different enough that the admissions committee will like it." We decided that she would be the country of "Helentopia" and her mother would be "Motheria." Her dad would be the "Fatherland" and her sister was simply, yet potentially powerfully, the "Sisterstate." It might sound kind of funny, but we actually drew a map of these countries on a piece of paper. Well, here is the finished product:

By Helen Cai, Duke University Class of 2014

For as long as I can remember, my world has been composed of four countries in a perfect state of harmony and disorder. My microcosm consists of Motheria, Fatherland, Sisterstate, and me, Helentopia. These United Nations constitute my world.

Motheria is Helentopia's most frequent trading partner in both manufactured goods and ideas. She is a powerful but understanding nation whose geographical proximity has succeeded in cementing her own perseverance and knack for comprehensive analysis into

Helentopia's internal policy. While we share similar traits, we also experience frequent skirmishes along our border. Tensions between our diplomats wax fiercely and often, but this has only sharpened my negotiation skills and made me rise to challenges. I still remember an early scuffle that demonstrates our dialectical relationship: I was six and we'd just moved to Germany from China, and I was so terrified that I refused to leave the house. Motheria made me face my ever-changing world by ushering me outside and demanding that I forge new international relations. Without Motheria's initial push and expectations, I doubt I would have transitioned so readily.

Fatherland and Motheria share a border along Rio Intelligentsia, but their similarities end there. While Motheria operates with cautious benchmarks, Fatherland prides himself on his extravagant dreams. He is the paradox that explains everything: one moment crowns him as the wise patriarch, another, the visionary businessman, and the next, the family's flour-coated chef. The fledgling Helentopia often snuck into Fatherland's conference chambers to observe the master of international relations at work. No philosophy, no topic is uninteresting to him. He would gesticulate passionately, voice quivering at the tragedy of the West Virginian miners or vibrating with the triumphs of the Beijing Olympics. At first, I merely watched his charisma from a distance but eventually came to participate in his debates.

Sisterstate is my satellite to the south. Although made a territory only seven years ago, she already possesses Chechnya's revolutionary intent. Sisterstate often mimics Helentopia's decrees, prompting me to set the best possible precedent.

Helentopia is my own realm. I differ fundamentally from Fatherland in terms of constitutions; he is conservative while I am liberal. I am not a true Motherian because my modus operandi is always unstructured. However, I weave my identity from their threads. My United Nations allow me to soar above language barriers, reach across cultures, and lead.

Adaptation and understanding are no longer foreign affairs to me after having lived on three continents: I revel in plunging into a constant flux of cultures and personalities. Down the road, I fantasize about serving as a delegate in the United Nations, setting forth resolutions like Motheria, winning sponsors by reason like Fatherland, and supporting my principles like Sisterstate does.

However, even if I never get to international relations, even if I never represent an actual country, my United Nations has enabled me to represent Helentopia. My physical world has always fluctuated Beijing, Frankfurt, Atlanta, LA but my world with Motheria, Fatherland, Sisterstate, and Helentopia, has always remained dynamically constant and nurtured my perception of the real world.

Evaluation:

Well, as you may have noticed Helen did not go to a UC but she was accepted into all the ones she applied to, yet ultimately chose Duke University. Regardless, this essay is AMAZING! I love the metaphor and the way she connected her family together through the UN metaphor. Not only does it reveal her family, and ultimately her, but it also ties in something that she is passionate about: international relations. An essay like this is definitely unique. Her writing style is impressive. She demonstrates a wide range of elements of effective writing. She talks about "trading partners" and about how her mother and father border the "Rio Intelligentsia." She does not write about how she and her mom fight; she writes about how Helentopia and Motherland have "border skirmishes" -- it's ultra-creative. Her sister is not a pain in the neck: she "possesses Chechnya's revolutionary intent." Impressive. So this essay may seem "risky" to some, using a UN metaphor to describe one's family, but it was well worth the risk, and the reward was college admission. This quickly became one of my favorite college admissions essays of all time. And it all started with a little bit of brainstorming.

8

COMMON ESSAY PROMPTS AND
HOW TO ATTACK THEM

Now that you have done a lot of brainstorming, and put a lot of thought into potential ideas for the essays, I recommend you try to match those experiences with the specific prompts you will have to answer. Look back at all of the brainstorming activities and all the stories you've listed and see if there are any connections. Did your "teacher/mentor" also help inspire you to become an attorney and go to law school (a goal for "5 years from now")? Did the "personal triumph/challenge" help change you from the "past" and help you achieve an "award/accomplishment" ?

Try to connect the dots:

- 5 years ago
- 5 years from now
- Awards/accomplishments
- Teachers/mentors
- Journal: Qualities you like about yourself
- Journal: Qualities you did NOT like about yourself

- Journal: How have you changed from the past?
- Personal triumphs or challenges
- 20 years from now

Since the prompts change at different universities from year to year, or at least from time to time, we're going to use the most common ones, and a variety from recent Common Application Questions as our first examples. I always tell my Advanced Placement English students that "AP equals answer the prompt" so let's attack some of the most common prompts from the "Common Application" and start to think about answering them in a personable and memorable way.

In the Common Application there are a wide variety of topics and angles that you could potentially pursue. And in this case, there is also an open-ended personal essay opportunity. Some prompts are very general, and others, like one on a character in fiction, are more specific. However, no matter how general or specific the prompt is for the college you are applying to, you must be as specific as possible. Remember your English teacher harping on your class to be more "concrete"? Well, concrete is memorable and vivid for the college essay. General is plain and forgettable in the college essay. Though your essay might not be completely unforgettable, the goal is to make it stand out enough that it will push you over the top. You want it in the short stack of students the committee is going to accept, not the large stack they are not going to accept. You can do it.

A "Significant" Experience

The point of most of these essays is to find a single salient experience that you would like to share with the admissions committee. This prompt is probably the most utilized across the nation. That's good news for you. You should not try to tell your whole life story in your admissions essay, but through all of the brainstorming and listing you have done for these essays, try to pick the *one* experience that you believe is most important. It should reveal something about your personality and character. If at all possible, the experience should either

41

highlight something that is <u>not</u> listed on your application, or provide a poignant and revealing story **expanding** on something that is listed.

Here is a great example from one of my greatest former students:

By Michael Danto, Harvard University, Class of 2013

"Let's try number thirty-five, across. The clue is, 'to resist authority.' The word is five letters. So far we have *r-e*-blank-*e-l*. Any guesses?"

Silence.

I stand before an audience of senior citizens. We are playing crossword puzzles. Exchanging glances, the other volunteers and I note the irony of the situation: an audience of teenagers would instantly know the correct answer, *rebel*. But these older men and women won't hazard a guess. 'Resist authority,' has melted away from the vocabulary here.

A brave soul named Winn shouts, *"Rebel!"* and everybody laughs. Winn is still resisting authority. She'll be one hundred in July. This is an unforeseen purpose of the Tesoro Reading Initiative, a service club I founded sophomore year—so that Winn, laughing and learning with her friends, could shout, *"Rebel!"*

Some say reading is dying. Every other week, *The New York Times* or *The Atlantic Monthly* publishes a eulogy of the book. Now that T.V. is ubiquitous, now that the internet is creating a paperless universe, now that BlackBerry's allow professionals to be permanently plugged-in, no one has time to read. Before performing any funeral dirges, society needs to discuss what can be done to avert this dystopian future. The search for deeper meaning, the exploration of worlds, the mystery inherent in life, the senses of personal growth and flux that are addressed in books will never die. Founding the Tesoro Reading Initiative, I aimed to nurture a community of writers, readers, and those born or yet to be born who may become writers and readers.

As the Tesoro Reading Initiative has evolved over the past three years, it has become my project and proving ground. In its first year, the Reading Initiative consisted of a few close friends and me. At the local Rancho

Santa Margarita library, we instilled our love of language in younger students through storytelling. Throughout my junior year, the club blossomed. It grew to encompass forty members and a variety of activities, such as reading news stories with high school special-education classes, playing crossword puzzles with senior citizens, and collecting books for schools, in addition to reading at local libraries. Rallying Tesoro's students, we collected two-and-a-half thousand books in our first drive. After delivering the books to Franklin Elementary, a school in an impoverished Santa Ana neighborhood, we read stories to classes for the rest of the day. A girl named Celeste approached as the bell rang. She asked, "Do you *really* like to read?" When I answered she said, "Good. Me too."

Leading up to the current year, the Initiative once more evolved. Now, in addition to the activities of past years, we host a foreign film series, called Reading the World through Cinema, at Rancho Santa Margarita library. The series examines foreign masterpieces, from eras and movements such as the French New Wave and Japanese postwar realism, with free screenings and open discourse. In the special-education classes, we not only read news stories, but also use conversation to teach appropriate behavior in social situations. Although we continue to play crossword puzzles with senior citizens, we also read classic short stories to seniors who have lost their sight. Their stories—about the Depression, about buying an Eisenhower jacket during World War II, about a boring summer job held in the distant past—reciprocate the stories we tell.

While volunteering, I have worked with extremes of life: the aged and the young, the mentally blessed and the mentally handicapped. On Mondays, in the special-education classes, I am forced to confront that some men and women, so different from how I am, struggle to adjust to an incomprehensible way of life. On Saturdays, at the senior center, I am forced to confront mortality. When Louis, a regular attendee, missed crosswords once, and we learned that he had passed away, the room was quieter than usual. His absence left something palpable in his place. Not exactly fear, but a similar emotion. On weekdays, at the RSM library, I have read "aloud," in sign language, to a deaf girl. Her mother picked books of signs off the library shelves for us to use. With the help of illustrations, the young girl and I learned to read signs together. When the mother hoisted the exuberant child onto her shoulders, the girl, tears welling in her eyes, blew the other volunteers and me a kiss. We returned her gratitude with waves and smiles. Another reader born, another job well done.

Evaluation:

Michael Danto chooses to focus his essay on one experience, his establishment of the reading initiative club. This is exactly what I suggest. There are at least two main reasons that this works particularly well for Michael: firstly, the single experience is perfect for revealing the type of person Michael is; and secondly, the single experience is perfect for revealing the type of writer and student Michael is.

Michael's essay truly captures his love of reading, compassion for others, and his leadership. He includes very specific incidents (the "rebel" example in the crossword) and these incidents reveal the big picture. He does NOT just try to give the big picture perspective or a nice summary of his club. Michael includes great snidbits of dialogue; for example, the little girl "do you really like to read" is very compelling. And though his particular experience seems pathos-driven, full of emotional appeals, it also reflects both his mature prose and his own personal maturity. He uses a higher level of diction than the average 18-year-old, and his syntax is varied, full of parallelism ("mentally blessed and mentally handicapped") and complexity, as well as simplicity – when simple will do. He is proud to help just one person want to read. That is what his club is all about. His opening draws you in, and his conclusion ties it all together…."another reader born, another job well done." The essay is full of images: the girls blowing a "kiss," the man named Louis absent, the Eisenhower jacket. These are memorable.

We can learn a lot from Michael's essay.

A Risk or Ethical Dilemma

Here's another potential essay where you can separate yourself from the pack. It is sometimes called "a risk or ethical dilemma" or sometimes the two are separated. Think about the past few years of your life. Have you taken a risk and started your own small business with a friend? Have you gone on a missions trip to Mexico to build houses? Read through your lists and scribbles from the brainstorming and see if anything rings a bell. Did you face an ethical dilemma in high school? Perhaps you were faced with a peer pressure situation of some sort. You were offered drugs or alcohol, and all of your friends were doing drugs or drinking? Of course this is common, but how you respond is what is going to be unique. Any dilemma or drama in your life that caused you to grow and learn from, can be expanded upon for an essay topic. Even if you feel you failed yourself at that moment, the story of your lesson learned could be a telling one of your own epiphany. It could have been a defining moment in your life. Be honest. Show how you GREW!

For the risk essay, as I like to call it, I have chosen to include Zack Guzman's, a former AP English student of mine who was admitted to Harvard University.

By Zack Guzman, Harvard University Class of 2014

The palms sweat. The knees shake. Teeth rattle, while the stomach rolls. There is no fear like the fear of failure -- this fear is surely not alleviated by a large audience, waiting like a monster to feast on a team's collapse.

I love this fear.

I love surprising people with the unexpected. It was the California State University, Long Beach High School Theater Festival, and my team and I were competing in Improvisational Comedy. Our school had never won, and I had only been on the team for barely two years -- expectations were low. The crowd knew it. The judges knew it. Their pencils held at the ready -- graphite waiting graciously to cast us aside as just another "improv" team that had mistakenly thought they were hilarious.

45

On that stage things were about to change. It was well lit -- every face in the audience lay painfully visible. Every smile, every smirk, every chuckle, every show of boredom. We had five minutes to give the best comedic styling we could muster. Tesoro High School was called, and it all began.

It was a quick five minutes, and at every second I could feel my heartbeat, the palms, the knees, the teeth, the stomach. Not only could I feel these tangible, adrenaline-altered organs -- but also I could see what fear had driven me to. It had driven my team and I to perform our best. Soon, having every face in the audience perfectly visible acquiesced from a curse to a blessing. The audience laughed, and the judges laughed harder. The applause echoed as my heart slowed. Fear had driven me -- but it did not control me. Through my many failures on stage I have learned it is one thing to survive five minutes in front of a crowd. But when you not only survive those five minutes -- when you leave the stage knowing it wants you to perform once more on top of it, knowing everyone in the audience agrees that you have won, knowing that you control fear -- it becomes an accomplishment, an experience.

Hearing Tesoro High School called out for first place in Improvisational Comedy not only made me proud because I knew we had won something for the first time in our school's history, but because I had won something for the first time in mine. I had proved to myself that I do not crumble under fear. At that moment I knew what I wanted to pursue, and now I find myself captain of the very same team I was on then. A captain who once thought his hands, his knees, his teeth had been shaking in fear-- but knows now that it was fear's hands, fear's knees, fear's teeth that were shaking in the midst of losing its control over me.

Evaluation:

This essay exceeded our expectations. Zack and I had brainstormed on how to somehow tie in a Comdey Sportz anecdote into an essay. And he does a wonderful job. I especially like the introduction and the conclusion. In the beginning, he hooks us with his imagery and his play on words. ("Teeth rattle, while the stomach rolls.") It's funny, and it draws us in. We can all relate to the "fear of failure" and this reflects the humility of Zach.

He uses the one sentence paragraph: "I love this fear." It's a perfect transition to his story of the improv. comedy competition. That brings me to the next point: once again, what makes this essay work so well is that it hinges around a story. That's our goal: to tell stories through our college admissions essays. I love his last line and his epiphany that it was "fear's hands, fear's knees, fear's teeth, that were shaking in the midst of losing its control" over him. It's a great use of personification and the conclusion ties in with the hook perfectly; the essay has now come full circle.

Diversity and You

"Boom!"

That is how a close friend of mine started her admissions essay for graduate schools. She told her family's story of leaving Vietnam during the war. Explosions were going off as they fled a war-torn country to come to America. Wow! Pretty amazing, ha? They came to America with the hopes and dreams of giving their children a BETTER start, all while fulfilling the American dream. She wrote this story for her dental school applications, and she was accepted into UCLA Dental School, one of the top dental schools in the country.

Now not many of us can write an essay about fleeing a war-torn country to live out the American dream. That is pretty unique. But we all have unique stories of diversity that we can tell.

Are you Caucasian? Well, this might seem like an essay topic that is NOT for you, but you might be wrong. Okay, so you might not have the dream story of your parents migrating from another country like my friend does. But, you probably have a great respect for diversity. Maybe you can tell a story of your best friend who is Korean or Chinese. You could talk about how getting to know them has opened your eyes to a new culture and new ideas about family and racism in our society. Or perhaps you have travelled overseas on vacation with your parents, and you went somewhere and you remember being the only "white" people at the restaurant or at the market. You may not have experienced "racism," but at the very least, at that particular moment, you experienced what it was like to be the minority. Perhaps that experience taught you something about what minorities go through every day in our country. As we already discussed, colleges want a community that is diverse, and they want members of the community who will respect and promote diversity. There are many ways you can express that.

Think about your contribution to what the Common Application calls the "educational mix." Further, this does not HAVE to be about racial diversity. You could write an essay about a certain quality or idiosyncrasy that makes you different, and how that can contribute to the larger diversity of a college or university.

The following is another essay by Haoxiaohan (Helen) Cai, a Chinese-American student of mine. She decided to write an essay about her Chinese name. Helen was accepted by Harvard University and Duke University – among others. She took a full-ride scholarship to Duke.

By Helen Cai, Duke University Class of 2014

"Haoxiaohan Cai."

Every name tells a story and mine is no exception. My name has changed several times as I moved from place to place – from China to Germany, from Germany to Georgia, and finally, from Georgia to California – and each variation signifies a leg of my journey. While my name was my most formidable hurtle to leap, it also granted me the lens through which I have perceived the dynamic world around me.

On April 24, 1992, a perplexed delivery nurse in Beijing, China must have held a pruny baby in her hands and wondered, "Haoxiaohan Cai? Who would name their child with four Chinese characters?"

My parents would. My unusual name drew me attention even in Beijing, where I grew up with my grandparents in a secluded village for elderly folk. Every morning, an old man in his *taichi* outfit would beckon,

"Haoxiaohan, tell us a story!" I would prattle on after his invitation; and I got quite good at it because the encouraging, wrinkled faces around me were the greatest audience a young storyteller could ask for. In turn, I was treated to the most gripping stories: recollections of bone-crushing tanks plowing through homes, of bitter hours spent waiting in the rations-lines in the blizzards of Beijing.

However, my halcyon days as "Haoxiaohan" did not last long. The advent of my new name came when my father's job uprooted us and deposited our family in a little German town.

The first day of elementary school in Germany was a veritable nightmare. I was six years old and was enrolling at a *grundshule* as its first Asian student. The golden-haired teacher went through the roll, smiling benevolently upon every Frederick, Timothy, and Natasha on the list – until her mouth caught on an aberration: my name. "Kay... Hio Sauer Huhn?" She pronounced cautiously. I snapped up to attention to salute the teacher but immediately shrunk down when I realized that nobody else had done so. By then, twenty-four pairs of inquiring eyes had fixated on me, as if they were expecting me to say something. Anything.

"Darf ich bitte zur Toilette gehen?" I offered helplessly. My mom had equipped me with three sentences for that day: "I am here, present," "Thank you," and "Can I go to the restroom?" In my panic, I had picked the last instead of the first. I was too flustered to care at that point, but the name "Sauer Huhn" (sour chicken in German) would become my nickname for the next two years.

It was not just "Sauer Huhn" that set me apart. I had to train myself anew in all the social customs and a new language: in Germany, you paid after you ate. You did not have to shove to snag a seat on the bus. You did not need to avert your eyes when talking with adults; instead, you impressed them by pressing your fingers against their palms in a firm shake – and passed some unspoken test of character. Through discerning little cultural tidbits from conversations I overheard, I began to speak my very own German words. Not only was I absorbing the history and diversity of Europe – in my small town, I was in fact contributing to it. I had to leave Germany and my stint as Sour Chicken after two years because my dad's job mandated another move. This time, it was to Atlanta, Georgia.

Another country, another language. Although English was easier to digest after German, it still took my third-grade teacher —a kindly, bespectacled lady, her relentless red pen, and countless hours spent after school in her classroom for me to overcome the language barrier. During our grammar sessions, she would not only instruct me on pronoun agreement but share vivid anecdotes about life in America. Just as the diversity of Germany taught me invaluable lessons, so did the diversity of the American South. Words such as "patriotism" and "chicken noodle soup" entered my vocabulary and "Haoxiaohan" evolved into "Helen." Helen was a nice fit for my name and also helped me fit *in*: I wanted a name my friends could pronounce, a name I would not be embarrassed to answer to.

Finally, we got transferred to Los Angeles when I was twelve. This time, there were no foreign words to hold me back and my confidence peaked. Words were no longer my obstacles; they became my liberators. Before I knew it, I was spinning in a vortex of dialogue and debate until I overcame what had once inhibited me.

Not all of my transitions have been this smooth, nor would I have wished it so. While my relocations were difficult, I am grateful for all the challenges I have had to face in adapting to foreign countries, because they have taught me about diversity. I am even more grateful that I can call corners on the opposite sides of the globe my home after conversing with their peoples, breathing under their skies, and loving their cultures. At seventeen, my international background has fortified me with experiences and insights that most people will not gain in a lifetime. Just like my name has changed with every location, so has my identity; I am more tolerant and have an insatiable appetite for different perspectives. After Sour Chicken, after Helen, I now come full circle to reemerge as Haoxiaohan.

Today, when someone asks me my name, I do not hide behind "Helen" any longer. I am proud of my diverse history and declare: "My name is Haoxiaohan. Hao – as in house. Xiao – as in show. Han – as in honey. There is quite the story behind *Haoxiaohan*…"

Evaluation:

Now, I know it's rare to include two essays from the same student in a book of this size, but Helen is a rare writer. The hook is great and it ties in perfectly for the diversity essay, but more importantly, she tells a great story. Not only is the story of her German slipup in elementary school hilarious, but it also transitions us to the woman she is today: flexible, resilient, and oh-so articulate. (Helen led the Mock Trial team from her high school to the finals as a senior.) As she puts it: "Words were no longer my obstacles; they became my liberators." There you have it.

Helen captivates the reader once again with her diction ("halcyon" which means peaceful) and concrete details as well. In Georgia, she learns from a "kindly, bespectacled lady, her relentless red pen…" Also, Helen is not afraid to use the sentence fragment: "Another country, another language." This is a nice topic sentence.

"Haoxiaohan" evolved into "Helen," she writes, and she guides the reader through that transformation. All in all, the essay serves many purposes in one: she expresses her diversity, she expresses her maturation, and she expresses herself. And it all hinges on a story from when she was six.

Furthermore, Helen does a nice job with parallelism and listing, as I suggested in the style chapter: "– from China to Germany, from Germany to Georgia, and finally, from Georgia to California…" This list mirrors the constant changing and moving Helen experienced. Then she has a clever shift in tone with: "'Haoxiaohan Cai? Who would name their child with four Chinese characters?' My parents would." The simple declarative sentence adds to the humor of the introduction, and the introduction is so important for grabbing the admission committee's attention (remember: they're going to read thousands of essays every year).

The best part of this essay though, and the most memorable is the story of her first day at school in Germany. It's a powerful anecdote not just because it's cute or funny, but also because it is indicative of the adaptability and resilience that Helen Cai has. That's what you want to do in your essay: yes, provide concrete details, and great anecdotes, but moreover, reveal your person, your character. In essence, her name change reflects her identity change. Helen writes a great essay about this change in her view of her own diversity.

In addition to Helen's essay, I have included an essay by another former of student of mine, Alejandra Benitez. Alejandra's father was a doctor and her mother was a chemist in Mexico before moving to America. Listen to Alejandra's story as it personifies the "American Dream."

"Diversity and You" Essay

By Alejandra Benitez, Brown University Class of 2014

My parents believed one thousand dollars would get them and my sisters off to a good start in the United States in 1989. Diapers and rent quickly absorbed one thousand dollars. My dad's job title changed drastically, from "doctor" in Mexico to "car wash employee" in the United States. My mom was promoted to McDonald's having been a chemist in Mexico. Juggling several jobs and raising two toddlers, my parents never stopped working. They work just as hard today to fulfill their one purpose for coming to the United States: the future of their three girls.

Growing up, I saw the medical books my dad kept as memorabilia on the shelves of our garage. Though I was intrigued by his world of medicine, I knew it was not mine. His excitement and passion for medicine, however, inspired me to seek my own interests. Placed in advanced classes since the third grade, I have been surrounded by diligent and ambitious friends, propelling me to earn exceptional grades like theirs. In high school, I marveled at our world's mind-boggling mechanics in anatomy and AP biology courses. I worked as an intern in the UCI department of ecology and evolutionary biology the summer before my senior year. To my proud parents, I was entering the field they find so prestigious, the one they pursued in college. At UCI, I observed the effects of dietary regulation on fruit fly populations and studied natural selection. I got a taste of working long hours in a lab as my parents have done for nearly twenty years. The things I learned in the lab made me question the devout Catholic faith I was raised with, the subjectivity of truth, and the microscopic miracles of science-- or of God? The people I met in the lab were inspiring, driven, and generous. My appreciation of people grows as I constantly observe how we impact others just as they impact us. I have seen my parents struggle and overcome obstacles. Knowing that other people are capable of doing the same, I am certain of one thing: I want to help the less fortunate progress.

The resources my parents have provided will allow me to search for the things I am passionate about. My family has never dipped its toes in the material wealth some of my friends possess, but I can swim in a fortune of encouragement and love, of rich culture, and of faith that my parents have poured out. They sacrificed a comfortable lifestyle, their beloved cultural roots, and their own families for their daughters. By choosing to come to the United States for my future, my parents have given me the opportunities they did not have growing up, and above all, the chance to decide what I want that future to be.

Evaluation:

What makes this one powerful is that it's such a powerful story. Of course not everyone has a story where their dad moved to America and left being a doctor to being a car wash attendant. That's pretty amazing. But Alejandra's writing is strong as well. I like her concrete details such as "effects of dietary regulation on fruit fly populations." I also like how she points out how she was always grouped with talented and exceptional kids and this really propelled her to success; this reflects how she's a team player and not just another egomaniac applying to the Ivy League. Alejandra is not. She's humble, intelligent, and articulate and that comes through in her essay. Admissions Committee members like confidence but not cockiness. Her conclusion is poetic as well: "My family has never dipped its toes in the material wealth some of my friends possess, but I can swim in a fortune of encouragement and love, of rich culture, and of faith that my parents have poured out." She includes a nice metaphor and again, this reflects the strength of her character. That is the goal. And she achieves it nicely.

By Krista Ward, Seattle Pacific University Class of 2015

There's this beige couch that sits in my parent's bedroom. It's old, worn and has been there as long as I can remember. It's adorned with grassy green pillows, bookmarked Bibles, clean clothes and sleeping cats. This beige couch has been home to my childhood, my adolescence, and I'm sure we'll meet again in the future. Tattered and sullied, the couch has been a place of tears, laughter, and stories that have filled my life with color.

My mother sat me down on that couch and told me the most amazing stories. She became the heroine in tales where I could see her battling all odds and leaving her home country of Guatemala to come satisfy her cravings for adventure. My mother's dream led her to a place where everything from the language to the lifestyle was foreign. I envisioned my mother as a firecracker, a woman not even five feet tall, with a strong Spanish accent, and big brown eyes that only wanted to capture everything she was experiencing. She told me of her fear, yet at the same time the great excitement at the realization that she had accomplished what she had set out to do. Yes, before me on the beige couch sat my mother, a pillar of strength, a woman of accomplishment, a mother filled with love and devotion. She said, "*Mija*, don't ever let anybody tell you what your limitations are. Go the extra mile. Follow your dreams and don't give up." These words became my inspiration for dreaming big.

My father grew up with the same beige couch. He is a devoted man, a man who worked hard for what he has; he is a workingman who doesn't take a vacation. Seeing him home on a Monday morning was something I rarely saw. It was Monday morning when, again, I sat down on that beige couch that has always been a foundation under my feet; it was there where my dad delivered the news of his unemployment. Yet, it was my father who came over to hold me and tell me that everything would be okay. I'm still not sure if his words were for me or himself, but either way, I remember the look on my father's face when he had to push aside his pride and let me know that for now, he couldn't provide for the family that he worked so hard for. Holding me in his arms, a man full of love and pride taught me that it was okay to be afraid. "In the face of fear

55

overcome the obstacles. Krista," he exhaled, "now is the time where we move forward." These words became my inspiration to prevail over all the barriers in life.

My grandmother, *Tita*, was visiting from Guatemala and we were sitting on that same beige couch where she told me a fairy tale. She began weaving a tale of a young girl growing up on a *finca*, a coffee plantation, and horseback rides through the massive fields of greenery. The fairy tale carried on when she met her Prince Charming, and their forbidden romance. He was once married and their romance was considered a bad omen, however they fell deeply in love anyhow. He took her away and married her in a small ceremony where their love bloomed and so did their family in a small home in Guatemala City. The tiny frail woman with unending faith sat next to me with an open Bible on the beige couch of stories and told me, "*Siempre vive para amar a Dios y a los demas.*" "Always live to love the Lord and love others." These words became my inspiration for living a life for God.

There's this beige couch sitting in my parents' bedroom. It's bedraggled and torn, but this beige couch contains the memories, stories, and words of wisdom that have shaped my past, present, and future. I know that this is the beige couch that I will be sitting on when I continue to map out my future stories that will hopefully inspire someone else's life.

Evaluation:

Aside from the obvious uniqueness of this essay topic, I love the personification of this couch: "I'm sure we'll meet again in the future." Krista also uses listing and parallelism artfully..."pillows, bookmarked Bibles, clean clothes, and sleeping cats." She provides powerful anecdotes of her mother, only balanced by her father's story, and her grandmother's story. It's all one fairy tale story of a magical couch that provides the perfect framing of her story – and her heritage. Krista uses dialogue, Spanish, and words of wisdom from her *Tita* to tell the reader her story – the story of her beige couch in her parent's bedroom...all the while, she tells the story of one slice of her life.

The Influential Person

Reflect back on all the people who influenced you not only in high school or middle school, but also throughout your life. Look back at the list of "influential" teachers or coaches from your brainstorming. Was there a coach who pushed you to a higher level? Did your history teacher inspire you to want to become a history professor? Did your English teacher inspire you to want to become a writer? Did your mom raise you by herself? Did your parents migrate from another country so they could raise you in America? How have they inspired you or influenced you?

Here is a sample from one of my past students who wished to remain anonymous. Certain identifying elements in her essay have been redacted. She was accepted into Harvard, Yale, MIT, Brown, and John Hopkins.

The Final Call

By Anonymous, Harvard University Class of 2014

Last spring, I saw a 40-year-old dream finally come to fruition. The scene will be forever embedded in my memory: a cascade of stage curtains lifted and a lone flute whirled through flurry of scales, beckoning the others to follow. The violins, the chimes, the choir joined together in harmony to answer this call; at the same time, youthful dancers canter out in traditional African garb, moving with their bodies, but also with their souls. Musicians with all types of exotic instruments entered, including a horse-headed fiddle from Mongolia and an ancient lute from Egypt.

Mesmerized by the throbbing beat and quixotic motifs, I stood on stage

entranced when the conductor gave me my cue. I quickly began to beat forcefully on the wire strings of my Chinese dulcimer, hoping the sound would mask the violent, nervous beating of my own heart. The audience can sense the anticipation and crescendo of the volatile dynamics inspired by the miraculous journey of a prophet in *The Final Call*. A dream to transcribe a fully orchestrated symphony encompassing universal harmony was finally manifested.

The mastermind behind the symphonic performance was my loving godmother I call "Granny T." A completely self-taught musical prodigy, she saw it as her calling to translate the revelation of universal harmony into a musical form. This was her way to fulfill a lifelong vision of uniting human beings regardless of race, color or ethnicity.

Granny T traveled the world to garner a cornucopia of traditional musical genres in preparation of this universal composition. Her particular interest in ancient Chinese instruments led her to my mother, an internationally known Chinese musician. Granny T still teases me about seeing my three year-old self "playing" the Chinese dulcimer when she first entered my home in 1995. After that visit, she fell in love with the instrument and wanted it to be the centerpiece in the *The Final Call* if it was ever performed as a full-length symphony.

I saw Granny T many times over the past fourteen years since my first encounter with her, each time enraptured by her worldly manner, her dignified aura, and radiant spirituality, and each time the *The Final Call* growing closer to its final form. I saw firsthand the development of her dream when I traveled with my mother to a performance of an early rendition in the Million Man March in Washington, D.C. Through this shared journey, I learned not only about the intricacies of music, but also a different world -- one of discrimination, hardship, and inequality. It was not until the September 11 attacks, however, that the project made its most significant strides toward completion.

Although still too young at the time to understand the complexity of world dynamics, I vividly remember her grave expression as she sat me down shortly after that tragic day, "America's heart is torn." I learned that tension and frustration penetrated the nation and the focal point of anger and spite descended on all Muslims, irrespective of their good deeds or commitment to their communities. They suddenly became the target of extreme prejudice and her organization underwent increased scrutiny. Granny T knew that this was a time that cultural unity was needed more than ever, an uplifting that only the magic of music could provide. Through all of this, she continued to guide me with a firm but caring hand. I recall her words, "pursue what you love and do not lose sight of your dreams..."

I have taken the sage advice of Granny T, both in the academics and in my true passion, music. By the time the *The Final Call* was ready as a fully orchestrated score for the Chicago performance, I had honed my musical abilities to be able to play alongside 60 professional musicians, fully cognizant of the fact that music has infused every nook and cranny of my life. Music is a powerful force, a medium for challenges to become inspiration. It has taught me not only the importance of the arts and harmony, but dedication and discipline to whatever I set my sights on. The passion I derive from the melodies and harmonies oozes into my entire being and is exuded in my personality, driving and inspiring me to reach new heights. Through determination and collaboration, Granny T accomplished her lifelong dream. Her words and music have taught me to never give up, so that I, too, can answer my *Final Call.*

Evaluation:

The writer shows off her impressive vocabulary a bit in this essay with words like "cornucopia" and "quixotic" but more impressive is her story of being inspired by a woman who had a passion for racial harmony and a passion for music. Although she probably could have included more, the brief dialogue of "Granny T" telling her "America's heart is torn" is both poignant and inspiring. The later quote of "pursue what you love and do not lose sight of your dreams…" also adds to the connection the reader felt with her mentor. And though this story is about a famous woman, the focus of the story is not on her, it is on how she directly impacted her.

She also does a nice job tying together the story of her learning this instrument so proficiently, and yet learning so much more about racial equality as well. Her final sentence and her play on the words of the title provide a perfect conclusion.

The next essay is another one that can easily fall under the umbrella of the "influential person" for the Common Application or the "Your World" essay if you are applying to a UC. In this case, this Korean-American phenomenon decided to write about influential *people* in her *world*.

By Jiyoon Cho, UCLA Regents Class of 2015

Paging Dr. Marvin Jung to Psychiatry.

On a bleak afternoon at the Ventura County Psychiatric Hospital, Dr. Jung observed his last patient of the day saunter in. The patient, glaring intrepidly ahead, slumped into the chair before gripping the edge of his seat. Routine questioning commenced and the patient's mental state visibly deteriorated -- beads of sweat trickled down his face as his body turned to stone. Without warning, the patient lashed out and bit into Dr. Jung's finger, leaving him to fend for a spout of blood.

My great uncle Marvin, despite the gravity of the incident, recalls it as one of many amusing events accrued within his trove of memories as a young psychiatrist. He inspires me with his composure. And don't worry – his finger is just fine.

Paging Dr. Sunhee Lee to Radiology.

Dr. Lee, the golden child that carried out her mother's dream of becoming a doctor, only analyzed the pictures, rarely discerning the stories behind them. When her mother sought her expertise on chronic low-back pain, Dr. Lee was left with a dilemma: act the part of compliant daughter or pragmatic professional. The weight of her mother's wellbeing lay in her hands. After thoroughly evaluating the X-rays, MRIs, and her mother's will against it, Dr. Lee consented and renounced the surgery.

My Aunt Sunhee attempts to reach beyond medical images to give her a better understanding of what is suitable for all of her patients, including my grandmother. She inspires me with her consideration.

Paging Nurse Marie Lee to Oncology.

Lady, a brain cancer patient, was re-admitted the same day Marie got promoted to head nurse of oncology. She claimed the title "Lady" for her grace and composure during the agonizing chemotherapy sessions. Watching Lady transform from a patient plagued with terminal illness to a caring wife and cheerful mother took Marie back to her father's hospital room twenty years ago. Afflicted by the final stage of lung cancer, Marie's father concealed his excruciating pain in an effort to be remembered not by his illness, but by his character.

My Aunt Marie connects with her patients. Most of her terminally ill cancer patients are so thankful for the lives they have lived, that they pass with the peace of mind that arises only from complete contentment. She inspires me with her bedside manner.

Paging Dr. Sharon Kim to Pediatric Neurology.

Everyone in the pediatric neurology department knows Dr. Kim as "the bunny mom." It all began a year ago when she met a new patient diagnosed with epilepsy. Dr. Kim, usually adored by her patients for her geniality, faced a new challenge in trying to communicate with the reclusive, withdrawn six-year-old boy. In order to capture his attention, she showed him pictures of the six bunnies she had rescued and fostered. Instantly, his eyes lit up, teeming with curiosity. Since then, Dr. Kim integrates her bunnies into conversations when meeting with apprehensive patients, engendering the title: "the bunny mom."

My cousin Sharon is always there, equipped with a contagious smile and generous warmth, to spread comfort. She inspires me with her sensitivity.

At my house, every family gathering is a general hospital meeting of sorts. Transcending esoteric medical jargon, the stories extend into the realm of humorous encounters, poignant memories, and unforgettable patients. Each one brings a unique perspective, specialty, and inspiration to me. Growing up surrounded by such captivating accounts, I have come to envision myself joining this expanding family hospital.

Paging Dr. Cho...

My calling is dermatology. I aspire to be an accommodating mentor like Dr. Jung, a conscientious guardian like Dr. Lee, a genuine caregiver like Marie, and an accessible friend like Dr. Kim. I want to join them in serving others through medicine. Gradually, I have learned the value of their success: dedication results from incorporating charm and passion into a sometimes-callous medical profession.

I imagine that someday, there will be a place in this specialized coterie, reserved just for me.

Evaluation:

Jiyoon takes a unique approach to describing her family in this "Your World" University of California essay and she also used this for her Common Application essay. Through her creative organization she is able to set herself up as the next doctor in her family of health care professionals. Each vignette of each family member provides a snapshot of some quality that she admires in them – and hopes to be able to emulate herself. Therefore though the essay describes the world around her, she simultaneously describes herself and who she wants to be. And she does so with tremendous creativity and style. Each anecdote ends with a strong declarative sentence: "He/she inspires me with…" This parallel structure throughout the story provides a perfect transition to her – and who she aspires to become.

Fictional Character or Historical Figure

Think critically about your favorite character in your favorite novel. Would this be a great opportunity to write an essay on that person? Would such an essay reflect you as a person? Maybe you were like Holden Caulfield at one point in your adolescence. The transformation from a Holden to the person you are now would make a great essay. And anyone on the committee who loves *Catcher in the Rye* would appreciate the parallel. Perhaps you took AP US History or AP European History and you became a Lincoln aficionado or a Napoleon Bonaparte buff. If you believe that your knowledge and understanding of this person helped influence you, then great. Particularly if your grades are not the strongest point on your application, this essay topic could be perfect for you. An essay about how reading the Frederick Douglass autobiography and its impact on you as an advocate for an end to racism in America would be a great fit. Give yourself an opportunity to show the admissions committee that you are an intelligent, analytical person – something they might not really believe just by looking at your grades.

At the same time, you must remember to link the person's life to your life. Remember, it's a college admissions essay. Show the parallels, what you saw of yourself in that character. They want to know more about you than the person you're writing about. It sounds paradoxical or confusing, but it's true. "We look for creative essays," Fritz Kuhnlenz from Boston University said. "The most common pitfall is that students spend the whole essay describing that character but don't link it back to them. They don't tell us why they chose that person. They forget that the application is about them."

Here's a sample from Justin Brown, a former student of mine, who fell in love with the book *On the Road* by Jack Kerouac. Justin was accepted into the UCLA Regents Scholar program, the University of North Carolina Honors Program, the UC San Diego Honors Program, and the University of Washington Honors Program.

By Justin Brown, University of Washington Class of 2014

Jack Kerouac's infamous break down in Big Sur killed me. His words, drenched in darkness and despair, felt so foreign compared to his enthusiastic, jazz-driven, almost child-like passion for the road and the unknown which it held. It was as if Jack's road had come to an end, and the grand revelation that he prayed would meet him never came. And there, at that beautiful Pacific, picturesque point, with the road behind him, there was nothing in front of him but an empty, incessant ocean. This somber end was an even worse beginning -- the beginning of the Beat King's demise.

I saw myself in Jack. I get it from my mother -- I'm an idealist, a romantic. Full of hope and full of passion. My vision of life and the unknown adventures that it holds keep me going in the darkest of times. I attach sentiment and meaning to the dull and meaningless. It excites me to know that each day I could be on the verge of some great adventure or some indelible experience. I have wanderlust. I am Jack Kerouac.

Yet, I refuse to follow the road of Jack Kerouac, one of my heroes. Kerouac couldn't take the brutal sting of reality, it was either his way or the highway (which just so happened to be his way.) When his friends, his family, life, and age abandoned him and his passionate dreams, he broke down and decided to live in the oblivion of drunkenness-- a place where his dreams might still exist. Instead, I find myself constantly adjusting to my new reality. I'm not a sell out; I still dream. But now I'm a dreamer who's ready to have a little battle with reality; and to win a battle, you must know your opponent.

Evaluation:

The section of Justin's text that is probably most poignant is when he writes, "I saw myself in Jack. I get it from my mother--I'm an idealist, a romantic. Full of hope and full of passion." I like this because here he ties in not only his connection to Jack, but also his connection to his mother. This reveals a lot about Justin's character to the admissions committee. At the same time, Justin also ends with a concession – that he is not exactly like Jack Kerouac – that he CAN take the road of reality. In this short essay, Justin aligns himself to the author nicely, yet he distinguishes himself as being somewhat different. Justin believes he is ready to "battle" reality.

9

COMMON PITFALLS AND FINAL THOUGHTS

The most common pitfall is not editing your essays enough. You want your final draft to be perfect – free from any errors. Remember, this is the first impression the admissions committee has of you. A few errors here or there can be interpreted as laziness or a lack of attention to detail. Your final drafts need to be perfect. This cannot be overemphasized. Your essay should be free from spelling and grammatical errors. Have your mom or dad read it. Read it aloud to yourself. Read your friend's essay and ask them to read your essay. Whether you planned and prepared and started writing the essays months in advance or you wrote them the day before they were due, your essays must be grammatically correct. If they are not, it will be a distraction, and it will hurt your chances for admission.

Another common mistake is inappropriateness. Fritz Khunlenz, from BU Admissions, warns student to make sure their essays are appropriate. "Remember to be appropriate....students want to wow us in admissions and some of the essays are just inappropriate. I have a whole pile of them from this year. I totally understand what they're trying to do. But at the same time, I tell students when I go around the country and visit applicants, show it to your parents. If your parents are proud of it, send it along. If your parents are not proud of it, don't." Again this ties into being yourself; if you are a humorous person, then of course, use humor. Just make sure it's appropriate. If you're not sure, ask a teacher to read it.

You don't need a title. Some of my samples include titles, but it is not mandatory. If you think of an amazingly creative title that is just perfect, then include it. If you can't, then don't include a title at all.

Also, when you decide what experience you are going to write about, avoid writing about high school-created experiences. For example, a whole essay about "discovering" your leadership skills in Student Government only tells the reader that a student leadership activity did its job. That is not unique. Can you write about your experience in Student Government? Definitely. Just make it unique to you.

Remember the essay is supposed to reveal more about you than just what can be read from a list of statistics and activities on the application. If you have revealed a glimpse into your personality, your dreams, and your life in your essays, then you have probably done a good job. Share the essays with friends not just for editing, but for answering this question. Does the essay reflect you? Do they come back with comments like: "This is great; it's so you" or "This really reveals your personality" then great. If they come back and say, "It's very entertaining" or "it's really funny" then that might not be enough. The goal is NOT to just be entertaining or funny; the goal is to reveal a deeper part of yourself than just some test scores and a transcript. If you do that, you will surely succeed.

The BU Admissions Officer summed it up this way: "Students are afraid to tackle difficult issues...want to have that wow essay but at the same rate they're shy about their situation. We need that active voice. If it's a scary situation, let it be scary. If it's serious, let it be serious. If it's funny, let it be funny. Many times they think they'll scare the admissions officer away...avoid the formulaic essay."

Always print out drafts of the essay. You will probably be able to catch so much more reading it on paper than on the computer screen. Remember to write in a way that depicts who you really are. Don't make the essays too much about the subject; always bring it back to you (this essay is all about you!). If an essay doesn't fit a prompt, don't be lazy and just try and recycle it. Trust me: they will know! Make sure the essay doesn't exceed the word limit. Some colleges have the limit as part of the directions. Not following this limit would mean you aren't following the directions. You probably will not make a good impression if you don't follow the directions. Make sure the beginning is unique and interesting. Don't be afraid to write what you feel.

Make sure the ending is unique and interesting. I can't emphasize that enough. Unique and interesting; that's you...now get it down on paper. Have fun and good luck!

10

SPECIFIC ESSAY PROMPTS & SAMPLES

The following is a compilation of some additional essay samples by former students of mine. Hopefully they will provide inspiration for your own writing – just as they have provided inspiration to me. Enjoy.

Prompt:

"Describe the world you come from and its impact upon you."

By Bhavik Vashi UC Berkeley Class of 2013

I don't come from one simple world. I come from two.

My life is a battle – a clash of two contrasting cultures. It is a war between traditionalism and modernism. As a first generation Indian living in Orange County [California], I have become a culmination of the old and the new, the conservative and the liberal, the intelligent and the creative; I am torn, yet I am complete.

Born and raised in India, products of an arranged marriage as teenagers, shipped to America: my parents are archetype eastern immigrants. I have a mother who washes our clothes, cooks our meals, cleans our house, prays everyday, and knows our calendars better than we do. I have a father who goes to work everyday, takes care of all the financial obligations, and provides us with an enviable lifestyle. My family is a stereotype.

Yet, I attend Tesoro High School located comfortably in the middle of Orange County. I see more Louis Vuitton purses than I do backpacks, students go to school without actually going to school, our parking lot looks like a BMW dealership, and sex, drugs, parties, and money seem to permeate their way into every passing conversation.

This makes for very interesting dinner table conversations. When I mention that I am going to a dance with a date, my mom reacts as if I just told her I was getting married. When I mention that the dance ticket costs sixty dollars, my dad makes me count how many other things could be bought for the same amount. When I tell them that I will be home by midnight, they both scold me for staying out two hours later than my bedtime. They're not kidding.

This is my world. With every passing day, whether major or minor, I am reminded of the ideological disconnect between the two biggest aspects of my life: my family and my social life. I am stuck in the middle of this gap, left to construct a bridge that appeases both sides.

Somewhere in this process, I have learned to love and appreciate different aspects of both cultures. Intertwining the two, I have created my own philosophy and personality and with these I am poised to pursue my future.

My family has kept me grounded. I have grown to appreciate my life and everything that I have. I have remained focused, using the morals and values of fiscal conservatism, honesty, and respect as my wall against distractions. I have committed myself to education and personal growth, so that I can someday do for my children what my parents were able to do for me.

Yet, I would not be complete without my school and my friends. Living life is every bit as important as appreciating it. The person I am today is so different from who I was eight years ago when I moved to California. A shy, nervous boy became an outgoing, free-spirited soul comfortable in his own shoes. I found myself.

My world has defined my perspective and my perspective sculpts my ambitions. To achieve the level of success that I have dreamt for in the world of business and economics, I will need the values and the hunger for excellence that my family has provided me with as well as the sociability and charisma that my school and friends have fostered within me.

My world is the foundation upon which I will build my pyramid of success. No matter how high I get, the only thing that will allow me to go higher is strength of my base – the clash between the two contrasting cultures with which I have grown.

Evaluation:

Bhavik's two worlds are a great contrasting paradox of each other. This provides the material for an outstanding essay. He also shows off his maturity of prose and personal maturity in the process. In what is really a simple organization, Bhavik discusses the complexity of the two worlds he is in. He calls his life a "battle – a clash of two contrasting cultures." This functions nicely as a metaphor and the use of the dash points to the paradox of his worlds. It's a good opening and a good use of more sophisticated syntax. The admissions essay reader will know exactly what the essay is going to be about, and the reader is drawn in to this intelligent essay through parallels such as "traditionalism and modernism." By the end of the essay, one has a great interest in the student's life – and world – and a great appreciation for him as a person.

One of my favorite essays from the summer of 2010 workshop, sprouted from the pen of one of Tesoro's best writers at the time, Nikki Mello. This essay was also used for the "Your World" prompt that the University of California schools ask for, as well as the "Diversity" essay from the Common Application.

By Nikki Melo, Texas Christian University Class of 2015

I live in Technicolor. Not in diversity but in an area where everything is vibrant and eye-catching -- a painting you must stop to look at.

The first color seen is orange. This is not just because this is Orange County, California but because it is also the skin tone of choice. A passerby's nose becomes filled with stench of the orange spray plastered on to the beautiful young girls while walking through the halls.

The next color on the canvas noticeable is green. America is affluent but Orange County is loaded. Even those at the lowest end of the spectrum have apartments that homeowners in other parts of the country covet.

The natural flirtatiousness of pink seeps into the students' eyes and lips. Everyone is young and beautiful, causing the sideways glances in class and silly little giggles at jokes that really aren't that funny. Seemingly innocent remarks hold romantic motives.

Yellow connects the outward appearances with the inside personality, making them grasp each other's hands. While many girls conform to yellow hair (naturally or otherwise), they also embrace their cavalier flippancy.

While all these colors swirl into one painting, there is an underlying color that scares everyone.

White.

Even with the rainbow of animated colors, white remains. A lack of color, something missing. Even with orange, green, silver, pink, and yellow, even with beauty, money, cars, lust, and fun, there is quietness. There is no substance. So many try to fill up their lives and find fulfillment. The fluorescent rainbow doesn't make people happy though. The rainbow simply covers up the cold, bare whiteness that many don't want to see. Everyone is trying to hide their original canvas, covering their true selves with distracting hues.

That's where I come in. I'm a color like maroon-- not the most popular, not the prettiest, not the color everyone reaches for. And I'm okay with that. I know who I am -- with the passion of red and the potency of black. The black that contains a contemplative seriousness -- one that illustrates a self-respect. I can say that proudly. While people may be afraid of the lack of color, I embrace it and fill in the corners. The white in my life is gone because I have found contentment in my own color, not in others. My peers may fit in a motel painting, with colors that will never let the canvas show. Meanwhile, I am on a journey to be displayed in the Met. Art critics can compare us all they want but I know what I am. I know I don't want to be orange, green, silver, pink, or yellow.

I am maroon.

Evaluation:

This is a powerful essay at many levels. The colors are a great metaphor not only for her "world," per say, but for who she is. Nikki also incorporates a series of subtle paradoxes to distinguish the subtle differences between her and those of many of her peers in So Cal. Orange County is orange because of the spray on tans, not because of the history of orange fields here. The apartments are so nice homeowners in other parts of the US would be jealous. Kids giggle at jokes that aren't really funny. The list goes on. "I am maroon" stands alone as a paragraph of potency, as does "white." She artfully used these to make them stand out. And Nikki does stand out in this essay, providing us with another great model to admire...in all of its beautiful colors.

The prompt:

"Only passions, great passions, can elevate the soul to great things."
(Diderot)

Describe one of your passions and reflect on how it has contributed to your personal growth. (500-700 words)

By Loraine Laguerta, UCLA Class of 2013

The heart-stringed angel many have christened, "piano." 88 identical keys in black and white sprawled shamelessly down the wooden plank, each note a different flavor. The combinations of keys are as coldly scientific as DNA coding, yet also just as gloriously precise. Move one key down and the bridal procession becomes an approaching train wreck -- move one key up and the solemn prelude transforms into sinister visions from a freakshow circus. When all building blocks of a song have fit into place, when passion mingles with well-disciplined technique, the results are breathtaking.

A song.

It is intoxicating. From the minute I hear it and for some time afterwards, it sticks in my head, an elating and unreasonably giddy feeling, my own personal charm for the rest of the day. I take pleasure in knowing that I am one of few to have stumbled on something so beautiful, yet I am not selfish. I want to share it with the world, I want terribly for others to hear it and feel the same way. I pity those caught in the doldrums but I leave them to their temporary amusements.

I put it away for fear of spoiling such a feeling, but when I take it out a second time, it is even more brilliant than the first. I am familiar enough to anticipate the rises and falls, but nowhere near desensitized. The pit of my stomach jumps, and a twisted knot pulls and loosens. It is painfully beautiful, and at this very moment in time, no one in the world can feel the composer's desires and tragedies as much as me. It is an incurable hunger that restrains itself because without restraint, the music loses its beauty. I put it away in patient anticipation for when my heart calls on it again.

Playing. The instrument is a man-made vehicle for the soul. To watch someone in performance brings out rose-tinted cheeks, in the performer and in her audience. The embarrassment of seeing someone bear her soul. The strangest way of knowing people, but by far the most intimate. When something moves me, and more than just me, I am no longer strangers with that person. It is impossible to be, after knowing that my emotions are affected in the same ways. Esa-Pekka Salonen cried while conducting the second movement of Jean Sibelius' Symphony no. 2. His audience, the ushers, the Swedish Radio Symphony Orchestra -- all became his closest, most intimate friends for that moment. He bared his soul to them, simply by going through the motions of music.

A song has a natural tendency to bring about closeness. Closeness in the camaraderie of an orchestra, in the mentoring of a student and a teacher, within the notes of the music itself and between the decorations surrounding it. The closer everything becomes, the more magical the single moment. Music has taught me closeness. Without it, I am mute. Reserved – shy at best, limited to a comfortable group of familiar friends and family. But by composing a single song, I am a storyteller. I am the improvisation keyboard soloist extraordinaire for the jazz band, the final piece of the puzzle of the first violin section in Tchaikovsky's "Serenade for Strings", the cheerleader of my niece (a fledgling piano virtuoso) and the grasshopper to my own teacher. I am the audience, witness to a miracle that so easily brings tears. I am connected – welded – to similar passions and emotions between people that have slurred together 6 billion strangers into 1 close and connected human race.

Music has made me fluent in one language understood by everyone.

Evaluation:

Loraine's essay is both eloquent and beautiful – just as her love of music and her composition of music is. This essays superbly displays her intellect. The admissions reader discovers instantly that Loraine is a thinker and a feeler. She thinks deeply and feels deeply about what she is listening to, composing, or playing. Her diction is poignant and her syntax is mature and purposeful. (She is "connected – welded – to similar passions...") Her interruptions and one sentence paragraphs effectively demonstrate her mature prose and her mature mind. The essay reads as a song. She plays the essay as she plays the piano. It is an intelligent essay, without *trying* to act intelligent.

Sample "Your World" Prompt

By Mikayla Wickman, Duke University Class of 2015

My family is a periodic table of elements. My elements include Mommium, Fatheron, Marcium, Gracium, and me, Mikaylon. Each is distinct but all are related; our family bonds are strong despite our less-than-perfect structure.

Mommium is a highly reactive solid; her family seeks solace in her solidity. Shortly after this element was discovered, she was adopted into a new family. Mommium nurtured a vast sense of curiosity about the family she never knew. It paid off. In 2004, she returned to her original family, her ground state, but not without the emission of photons and elbow grease. She fearlessly befriends members of any group, forming bonds that time or distance cannot break. Scientists marvel at the loud chortles given off when she is delighted or amused. She effervesces with joy in even the most unfavorable conditions, and this joy attaches itself to all she comes in contact with. When she gives, she is positively selfless, inspiring me to do the same. Found in flower shops and discount stores, the waves of influence created by Mommium penetrate even the hardest of hearts.

Fatheron is a noble fellow. Discovered along the Great Lakes, he is the eldest boy in a family of eight elements. He takes great interest in nuclear science: he has worked at a power plant for over twenty years. Fatheron and Mommium collided in 1990 and it was instant chemistry. Try as he might to stay with Mommium, Fatheron's marital bond with her was broken three years after it was formed. He never formed another bond. Fatheron belongs to an underappreciated group—other elements often take for granted both the energy he exerts to remain stable and the hand he willingly lends to his thankless friends.

Mikaylon was discovered in 1993 in California, while Mommium and Fatheron's bonds were still intact. She is liquid at room temperature. Though she moves around a lot, she was not born with the bravery of a gas. Her instincts tell her to be hesitant to bounce off walls at great speeds, though she ceaselessly adapts to new situations and containers. As a river flows, with it she goes. As a tide rises and falls, her mood does the same. She turns to steam only at high temperatures and does not freeze easily when her environment grows cold. Periodically, Fatheron and Mikaylon bond at the dinner table. His passion for science manifested itself in Mikaylon over the years and grew like a benevolent virus in the very core of her being.

Marcium is a nonmetal. He acquired a second name, Stepdaddium, thirteen years ago when he joined the table. As the old saying goes: opposites attract. He came in contact with Mommium and they bonded immediately. No catalyst was necessary this time; their connection was natural. A few years later, Mommium and he joined together formally with two carbon rings on a rainy day in April. Marcium's affinity for all things technological sparked wonder in Mikaylon: '20 Questions' became an understatement. She found out through her incessant interrogations that he liked to create, to invent, to make the world an easier place to live in. In the midst of bonding with Marcium over Discovery Channel shows like Mythbusters and How It's Made, Mikaylon dreamt of the ways she might one day influence the world through her creations and ideas. The dream continues to this day. Meanwhile, a new element was discovered that replaced Marcium as the newest addition to the family.

Gracium is a powerful solvent to which Mikaylon is the solute. Every word, every habit, and every action Mikaylon emits is dissolved into Gracium, from the Converse shoes they both wear to the funny faces they wear as distractions during staring contests. Mikaylon soon learned to emit only good words, good habits, and good actions. Mikaylon and Gracium's seven-year age difference keeps their encounters generally explosion-free. Spending time near Gracium helps remind Mikaylon that the universe is not composed of only Mikaylon atoms.

Mikaylon's collisions and embraces with these elements have changed her. No longer is she a single atom of a simple element. As a caterpillar cannot become a butterfly without a safe cocoon and a profusion of patience, Mikaylon could not have developed into the complex individual, the multi-faceted compound, without Mommium's infectious laughter, Fatheron's quiet intelligence, Marcium's practical innovation, Gracium's unwavering admiration and seventeen years of cultivation. Mikaylon dreams to inspire other atoms to break out of their electron shell, just as her family inspired her.

Functionally dysfunctional, this periodic table of organized chaos will be my life-long guide in times of confusion and it will be my source of strength when I feel weak. Most of all, it will be my road map for the journey ahead.

Evaluation:

Mikayla's creativity and love of science permeate through this metaphor for her family and what has shaped her. Structurally, it is simple; each paragraph comprises an element, which represents an influential member of her family. Artistically, it is brilliant; the way she tells about her parent's divorce and the way she describes the connection to her little sister are all done in innovative, brilliant, and unique ways. I also love the way her father was "discovered in the Great Lakes" and how "opposites attract" between "Mommium" and "Stepdaddium." The best part of the essay however is the way she ties it all together with the caterpillar analogy and the way she articulates the "multi-faceted compound" that she has become today. Overall, its a fantastic scientific essay!

Sample Essay to the University of Southern California (USC) for 2009

By Lyn Cowan, University of Southern California Class of 2013

I love to be stressed. Within the whirlwind of chaos that stress tends to create, my mind settles into a serene state. All of my friends called me crazy when I let them in on my personal epiphany, but I believe being stressed is necessary to my normal functioning—sort of like how Ritalin is necessary for a person with severe A.D.D. Instead of Ritalin, however, my drug of choice is the activity I throw myself into; I love the Theatre Department, I love being a student theatre critic, I love working on student government, I love to play the piano, I love to dance, I love to take ridiculously difficult classes. See what I mean? Thankfully, my addiction happens to be something that is self-constructive rather than self-destructive.

I do not deny the fact that my desire for stress is probably a weird psychological condition that needs to be addressed. But the real question is: How did I come to be like this? From the time I was very young, my parents encouraged me to try a variety of different activities. This incredible love and support from them resulted in my many areas of interest. When it comes to choosing the fall play or coordinating a Homecoming float—I can't. Or deciding between taking AP French IV or AP Literature— I can't do that either. Some unknown part of my brain speaks to me. It says, "It's not that much. Do it all! You know you'll regret it if you don't…" That little voice is always right. The number of activities I participate in (no matter if I enjoy them or not) and stress are directly correlated. Due to the fact that I love participating in numerous activities that suck up all of my free time, I have adapted to stress and even grown to like it.

If I'm not stressed, then I worry. Stress is generally my indicator of productive behavior. The more stress I have, the more I accomplish. This idea dawned on me one day when I had just finished watching my 10th consecutive episode of *America's Next Top Model*. Life was good—I had nothing to do but simply relax. Relax… ? What good does relaxing by means of mind numbing reality television ever do anybody? None. Sure, watching stick-thin amateur models parade around nourishing themselves with nothing but carrot sticks is funny. It gave me a new appreciation of my favorite food, ice cream. But after watching TV all day, nothing had come out of it; there was nothing rewarding about it. I would much rather wake up at 5:30 in the morning to go to 0 period, go to all 6 of my other classes, go to a two-hour play rehearsal, and then come home and do my homework than sit and watch TV all day. If I wanted to be a couch potato, I could have very easily been a dog instead of a human: Dogs sit around and watch the world whiz by them every day. But why waste my superior human mind and opposable thumb? I am a human for a reason and I thoroughly intend to take full advantage of it.

So, don't call me crazy. Call me ambitious, call me driven, call me dedicated, call me focused. Just don't call me crazy. I'll concede, all of the happenings of my life do make me stressed. But stress acts as my personal barometer of success! Machiavelli famously said, "The ends justify the means." So if that means I have to be stressed to get myself somewhere in this world, I'll take the stress and run—loving every minute of it along the way.

Evaluation:

Lyn did a fantastic job in this essay revealing herself. By discussing one single topic, stress, she is able to reveal many things about her character, her drive, and her motivation. This is all very persuasive. It is also a great technique. She takes something negative and something that could be viewed as a weakness, feeling stress, and turns it into a positive. Obviously there is going to be some amount of stress in college: juggling research papers, midterms, final exams, being away from home, dealing with a roommate, managing a social life, and the general pressure of being on her own for the first time in her life. Any admissions committee knows that if she thrives on stress and she excels under pressure, then she has a greater chance for success at their university.

Stylistically, Lyn uses the shorter, simple declarative sentence sandwiched next to the longer, compound-complex sentence, and those short ones are packed with power. "I love to be stressed," she introduces herself and the paradox of her life. "So, don't call me crazy," she tells the reader in the conclusion. Lyn probably could have used this technique even more, but another potent and powerful aspect of her style is her parallelism. "Call me ambitious, call me driven..." she asserts her strength of character and her strength as an applicant to that university.

The best thing I like about his essay is her sense of humor. She makes fun of others a little, but most of the time she makes fun of herself. I love the self-deprecating humor. It reveals her personality. She's real. Well done.

Sample Essay for the Common Application

Four Walls, Four Years

By Carly Eubanks, Cornell University

Freshman: Eyes downcast, I nervously shuffle to English class, as the hordes of upperclassmen stampede, trampling my already distraught demeanor underfoot. I enter the classroom and take my seat in a taut plastic chair, tinted a shade of maroon reminiscent of the favored "Mulberry" crayon of my childhood. Mrs. Willett grins as she welcomes us to our high school hell, eerily warning of the walls which resemble the pallid color of a "caucasian cadaver." At this lumbering, uncomfortable stage of life, I do not foresee that this color of decay will surpass the realm of those four walls.

Sophomore: Satiation surges through me as I beam at the Wolverine Pop Warner Cheer Team, each member eclipsing her mental or physical handicap with a display of untamed zeal. Mid-cheer, the eleven-year-old Aiden prances off to grab the hands of strangers, enthusiastically saying "Hi-ya!" in a voice that swaddles innocence. She is uncontaminated by worldly cruelties, yet she is fragile, and her underdeveloped bones forecast uncertainty. It is this uncertainty that sucks the cadaver-colored walls towards me, like paper clips to a magnet.

Junior: I trudge up five flights of stairs, wearing a stiff navy polo with the embroidered "Mission Hospital Volunteer" covering the left breast. I wait four seconds for the "automatic" doors to grant me entrance to the post-surgical floor, where I will begin my shift. During the next four hours, I face lonely people, bitter people, sanguine people, agonized, terrified, paralyzed-with-pain people. Amidst the 6 o'clock meal deliveries, I am shaken from the typical pattern of patient interaction as I enter a particular room. Meal tray in hand, I poke my head beyond the sullen blue divider curtain, and my eyes fall upon a blanched patient. Machines, tubes, and despaired expressions gather around the middle-aged woman. The cadaver-colored walls shrink, once again suffocating me with brutal reality.

Senior: I am 9,000 miles from home, standing in the mud-walled home of a Rwandan in the remote village of Byumba. I stare into the sallow eyes of Odette, who is HIV positive and struggling to raise her six children. She confesses her physical and emotional pains, seeking solace. I race through my brain, scan stacks of knowledge, rake through scattered thoughts, trying to unbury some shrapnel of hope that can bind her wounds. My efforts are futile. Her disease and her qualms are incurable to my untrained mind. Crashing upon me are the dreaded walls, teasing me, taunting me, reminding me that illness is imminent, and approaches some sooner than others.

I keep Aiden and the ailing patient and Odette in my spirit. I color the cadaver walls a deep shade of Mulberry and tune my mind to the sweet hymn of realized aspirations: that one day I can be a bearer of cures, a "Doctor Without Borders."

Evaluation: Carly takes the classification/division structure to a whole new level with this poignant essay. Stylistically, she has just about everything you can in such a compact, yet powerful personal statement. I can picture the image of Mrs. Willet's grin and love the analogy of the "caucasian cadaver." Poetry resounds in her line: "It is this uncertainty that sucks the cadaver-colored walls towards me, like paper clips to a magnet," as the metaphor extends. In her junior year, she employs the power of listing. Then she grabs you with the cacophony of "suffocating me with brutal reality." By senior year, you realize that she is not content playing doctor wannabe in her safe bubble, but her eyes are on the globe, and though just a teenager from California, she has already been to the far reaches of that globe to help the sick. Carly artfully combines the concrete (the "eyes of Odette") and the abstract ("shrapnel of hope"). So, yes, stylistically, her essay is strong, but most importantly, the effect of her experiences on her as a person, a woman, and hopefully a future doctor, make lasting impressions on this reader.

Q & A for a UCLA College Essay Reader

MM: What are the most common mistakes you see with college essays you've read?

UCLA READER: **Regurgitating what's already on their application is the MOST common mistake. The second is talking about things that are personal to them but are very common—like a divorce, a medical issue, or a death. They can talk about these things, but they have to talk about how they have <u>changed</u> them.**

MM: What is the main thing you look for in the college essay?

UCLA READER: **Because essays are value-added, do I have a better picture of who this person is or is this a missed opportunity – that could separate them from someone with a similar GPA, similar background, and similar activities?**

MM: How important is writing style in the college essay?

UCLA READER: **Write it as personally as possible – adding to the holistic review of the person. If the style can tell what type of student she/he is then that can be value-added.**

MM: On the question about "your world," how abstract or concrete do you like students to be?

UCLA READER: **Some students are better at the abstract. The better the writer, it helps usually makes the essay more compelling. Meanwhile, the concrete can be good too.**

MM: For the question on their talent or achievement or personal experience, what do you view as more important: the experience or the EFFECT of that experience?

UCLA READER: **A little bit of both is needed. If the experience is not unusual – unless the kid is an Olympian or something – and I have read essays from Olympic athletes, then effect is more important.**

MM: Is it considered taboo to talk about failures in a college essay?

UCLA READER: **No. If there's that silver lining, and they have changed.**

MM: How crucial are length and following the directions?

UCLA READER: **That ties back to missed opportunity. It should not be too short, nor too long. You want to get across the whole person.**

*Author's note on the new University of California essays:

If you are reading this book and are applying to the UC's in the fall of 2016 or beyond, the prompts have changed and the word count has changed. Now you pick 4 of 8 prompts and write less (350 word max for each).

A lot of these prompts have similarities to the old prompts, so the same principals apply that I have outlined in this book. Part of the goal of the new UC prompts is to get you focused less on just your own personal achievements for your own personal achievement sake, but to articulate how your personal achievements have positively affected the world around you. Keep that central as you work on your shorter responses. Demonstrate to UCLA or Cal or wherever you're applying that your personal success has benefited your school, your family, or your community – not just you.

I spoke to a UC reader and she suggested that students convey how their accomplishments have made an impact on the "public good." Do this in the 4 prompts you select, and you will truly impress the UC readers. Best of luck everyone!

- Mark Mooney

Made in the USA
San Bernardino, CA
09 June 2018